D1161122

The Cranky Crocodile

Story by Rebecca Johnson
Photos by Steve Parish

GARETH STEVENS
GS
PUBLISHING
A Member of the WRC Media Family of Companies

Please visit our web site at: www.garethstevens.com
For a free color catalog describing Gareth Stevens Publishing's list of high-quality books and multimedia programs, call 1-800-542-2595 (USA) or 1-800-387-3178 (Canada). Gareth Stevens Publishing's fax: (414) 332-3567.

Library of Congress Cataloging-in-Publication Data

Johnson, Rebecca, 1966–
 The cranky crocodile / story by Rebecca Johnson; photos by Steve Parish. — North American ed.
 p. cm. — (Animal storybooks)
 Summary: A crocodile that has lived peacefully with the other creatures at her watering hole suddenly becomes mean and drives them all away.
 ISBN 0-8368-5970-7 (lib. bdg.)
 1. Crocodiles—Juvenile fiction. [1. Crocodiles—Fiction.] I. Parish, Steve, ill. II. Title.
PZ10.3.J683Cr 2005
[E]—dc22   2005042633

First published as *Cranky Crocodile* in 2003 by Steve Parish Publishing Pty Ltd, Australia.
Text copyright © 2003 by Rebecca Johnson. Photos copyright © 2003 by Steve Parish Publishing.
Series concept by Steve Parish Publishing.

This U.S. edition first published in 2006 by
Gareth Stevens Publishing
A Member of the WRC Media Family of Companies
330 West Olive Street, Suite 100
Milwaukee, Wisconsin 53212 USA

This edition copyright © 2006 by Gareth Stevens, Inc.

Gareth Stevens series editor: Dorothy L. Gibbs
Gareth Stevens cover and title page designs: Dave Kowalski

Printed in the United States of America

1 2 3 4 5 6 7 8 9 09 08 07 06 05

Mrs. Crocodile was fierce-looking.
She had a huge mouth
and big, sharp teeth.

She lived in a water hole,

which she shared with many other kinds of wildlife.

5

Birds and beasts alike had lived side by side with Mrs. Crocodile for a long time.

6

And most
of them felt safe
around her.

But, lately, something seemed to be wrong with Mrs. Crocodile.

She was mean,
and she was nasty.

"Get out
of the water!"
she snarled
every day.

"I'll eat you all up
if you don't stay away."

When birds tried to fly over the water hole, Mrs. Crocodile scolded them with a **SNAP!**

SNAP!

SNAP!

SNAP!

13

The turtles said, "We have seen enough.
That crocodile is much too gruff."

"This water hole's no place to stay." Then, the turtles ran away.

15

What the other animals didn't know was that Mrs. Crocodile was hiding something.

Each day, after chasing
all the animals away,

she would sneak
back to her nest . . .

and call softly,
"Come out now,
little ones."

Suddenly, small crocodiles appeared! Carrying them gently between her big, sharp teeth,

Mama crocodile took her young to the water hole.

"There now," she said to her sweet little dears.

"You're all safe with Mommy.
There's no one else here."